From Your Friends At The MAILBOX® *Magazine*

"Look What I Wrote!"
Student-Made Accents For Creative Writing

Grades 1–3

Ideas By
Cheryl Stickney

Product Development Manager
Kathy Wolf

D0774955

Editor
Ada Hamrick

Copy Editors
Carol Rawleigh, Gina Sutphin

Illustrator
Donna Teal

Cover Design
Donna Teal

©1995 by THE EDUCATION CENTER, INC.
Reprinted 1996
All rights reserved except as here noted.

Table Of Contents

How To Use This Book

Motivate your students to produce their best creative writing with these seasonal displays! Use the finished projects to create terrific student-made bulletin boards or send them home for Mom and Dad to proudly show off on the refrigerator!

For each project in this book, you'll find a literature selection to introduce a creative writing topic and a suggested writing activity, such as a haiku, an acrostic, a short story, or a letter.

Reproduce the accompanying patterns for each project and gather the materials listed. When students have completed their writing, direct them in assembling the paper accent to display their work.

(Note that some projects require student work to be mounted on the paper accent. Be sure to provide students with paper of the appropriate size to fit each pattern.)

Literature Selections

Book Title	Author	Publisher
Will I Have A Friend?	Miriam Cohen	Aladdin
Liar, Liar, Pants On Fire!	Miriam Cohen	Dell Publishing Co., Inc.
Happy Birthday, Dolores	Barbara Samuels	Orchard Books
Detective Mole And The Halloween Mystery	Robert Quackenbush	Little Simon
That Terrible Halloween Night	James Stevenson	Greenwillow Books
How A Book Is Made	Aliki	Crowell Junior Books
A Turkey For Thanksgiving	Eve Bunting	Clarion Books
The Song Of The Christmas Mouse	Shirley R. Murphy	HarperCollins Children's Books
Rudolph The Red-Nosed Reindeer	Robert L. May	Applewood Books
Un-Happy New Year, Emma!	James Stevenson	Greenwillow Books
Bob The Snowman	Sylvia Loretan	Viking Children's Books
The Tooth Witch	Nurit Karlin	Trophy
A Garden For A Groundhog	Lorna Balian	Humbug Books
The Valentine Bears	Eve Bunting	Clarion Books
President's Day	Laura Alden	Children's Press
Leprechauns Never Lie	Lorna Balian	Humbug Books
Sylvester And The Magic Pebble	William Steig	Simon & Schuster Books For Young Readers
Round Robin	Jack Kent	Prentice Hall
The Easter Egg Artists	Adrienne Adams	Scribner Books For Young Readers
The Mother's Day Mice	Eve Bunting	Clarion Books
Happy Father's Day	Steven Kroll	Holiday House, Inc.
Henry's Fourth Of July	Holly Keller	Greenwillow Books

CLASSMATE SLATES

These old-fashioned slate boards will help your students get acquainted at the beginning of the year. Reproduce the patterns on pages 6 and 7 for each child. Gather the materials listed below. Read *Will I Have A Friend?* by Miriam Cohen or *Liar, Liar, Pants On Fire!* by the same author to your students. Discuss the fears, expectations, and questions students may have on their first days of school.

Assemble the slate boards; then have each child write his name, age, and his favorite food, hobby, sports team, TV program, or movie star with a piece of chalk. Have students exchange slate boards. Tell each child to find out three things about his classmate and report to the class. After everyone has shared something about his new friend, mount the slates on a bulletin board with the title "We're Getting To Know You!"

Materials:

9" x 12" sheet of brown construction paper
8" x 11" piece of black construction paper
girl/boy patterns on white construction paper
crayons
scissors
glue
piece of chalk

Directions to the student:

1. Cut out the girl or boy head and hands patterns, and then color to look like you.
2. Center and glue the black paper on the brown paper to make a frame.
3. Write your name, age, and a favorite thing on the black paper.
4. Glue the head and hand patterns to the slate as shown.

Head Pattern

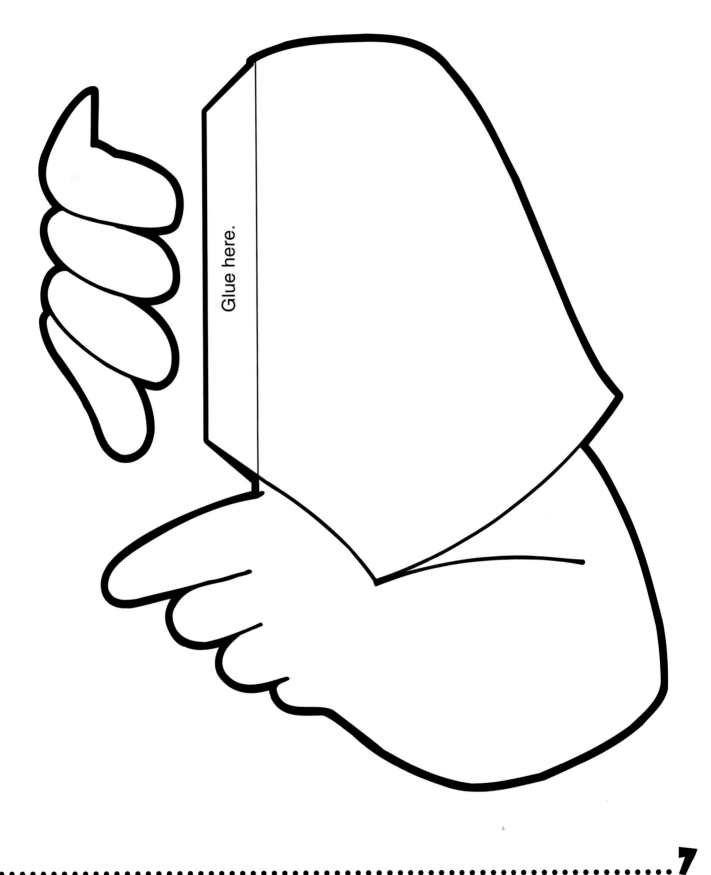

Glue here.

BIRTHDAY TRADITIONS

Donna
April 7th

The special tradition I look forward to is baking a cake, frosting it, and blowing out the candles!

This delicious display will remind you of class birthdays all year long. Read *Happy Birthday, Dolores* by Barbara Samuels, the story of a very active little girl and her birthday party. It's full of disasters and very memorable! Have students think of traditions that mean a lot on birthdays. Have each student write a paragraph describing a special tradition she looks forward to on her birthday.

Then have students create the birthday cake paper topper using the patterns on pages 9–10. Mount the cakes and papers on a wall or bulletin board with the title "When Do We Blow Out The Candles?"

Materials:

icing pattern on colored construction paper
cake pattern on white construction paper
plate pattern on colored construction paper
candle patterns on colored construction paper
gold glitter
scissors
glue
crayons
stapler (optional)

Directions to the student:

1. Cut out the icing, cake, plate, and candle patterns.
2. Glue the icing to the top of the cake pattern.
3. Choose a number of candles to represent your age.
4. Add a glitter flame to each candle. Glue the candles to your cake.
5. Glue your cake to the plate cutout.
6. Write your name and birth date on the cake.
7. Glue or staple your paper below the plate.

9

Candle And Plate Patterns

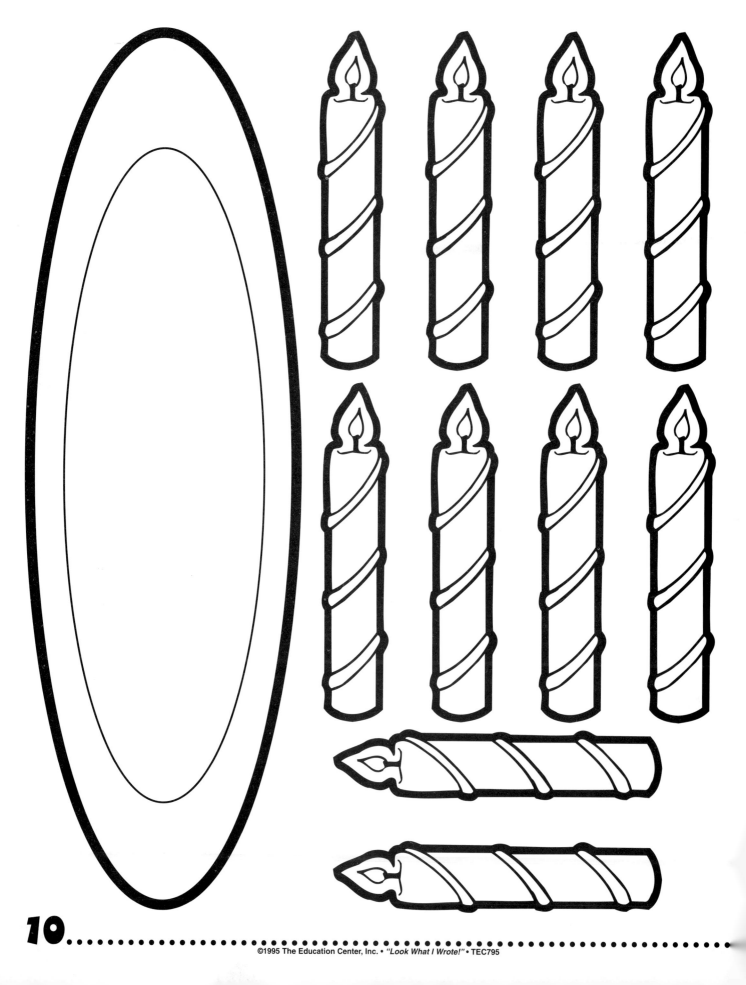

PUMPKIN-PATCH KITTY

Create a pumpkin patch of cute kitties to highlight students' good work. Share *Detective Mole And The Halloween Mystery* by Robert Quackenbush with your students. All the jack-o'-lanterns in town are stolen, but Detective Mole discovers the culprit in an old haunted house. The thief turns out to be a witch's lost cat who is trying to leave a signal for the witch when she flies by on Halloween. Detective Mole and his friends help the cat leave a giant message for the witch.

I think the witch and the kitten would fly to the pumpkin patch to plant seeds for next year's jack-o'-lanterns.

A Pumpkin Patch Of Good Work!

Ask students to imagine where the witch and kitten might fly. Then have students write about the adventures of the kitten. Using the patterns on pages 12–13, create the paper frames to highlight their stories. Duplicate the kitten head, paws, and tail on tagboard and cut them out, creating templates for student use. Mount the finished projects on a wall or bulletin board with the title "A Pumpkin Patch Of Good Work."

Materials:

pumpkin pattern on orange construction paper
tagboard templates of kitten head, paws, and tail
black construction paper
green construction-paper scraps
scissors
glue
white crayon

Directions to the student:

1. Cut out the pumpkin pattern.
2. Cut out and glue on a green paper stem.
3. Glue your paper to the pumpkin.
4. Use the templates to trace the kitten's head, paws, and tail on black construction paper. Cut out the pieces.
5. Glue the kitten head, tail, and paws to the pumpkin.

Pumpkin Pattern

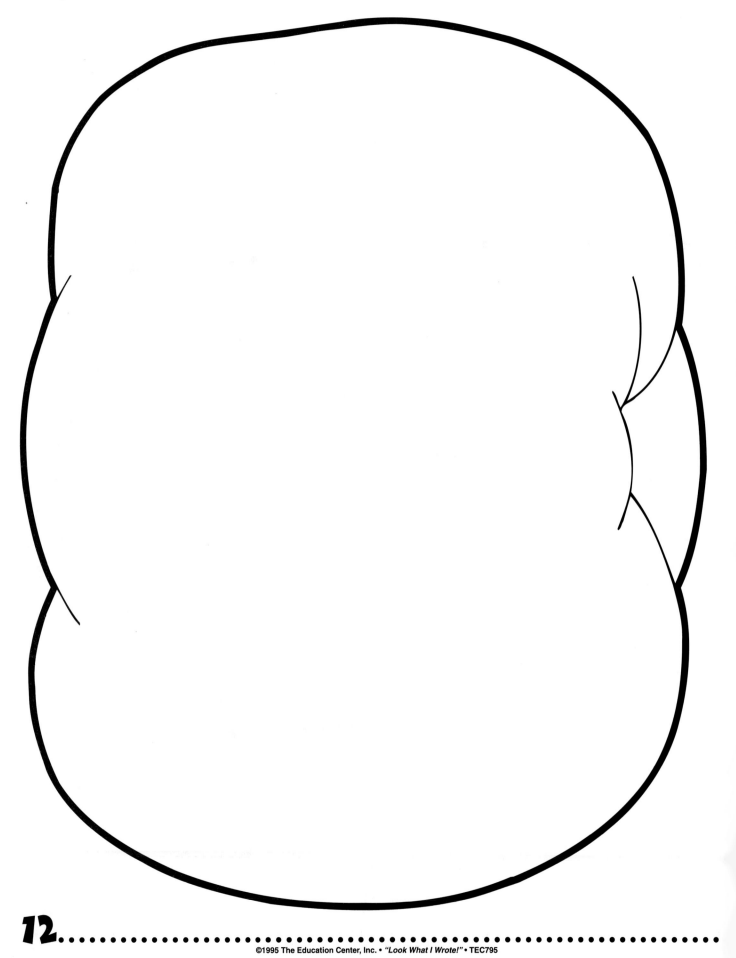

12

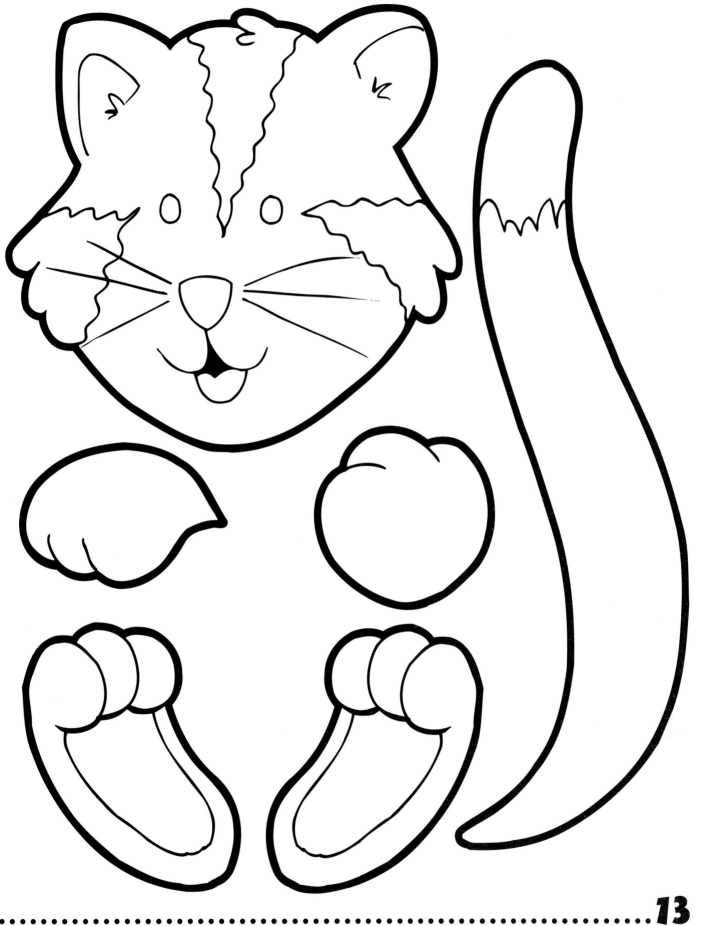

13

HALLOWEEN HOUSE

It was a dark and scary night. The moon made shadows that looked like hands.

Show off scary Halloween tales with these haunted houses. Share *That Terrible Halloween Night* by James Stevenson with your students. Grandpa tells Mary Ann and Louie what happened to him when he went into a strange house one terrible Halloween night.

Ask students to write stories about a haunted house and the happenings there on Halloween. Then have each student create a ghostly haunted house using the patterns on pages 15–16. Display the houses on a bulletin board with the title " 'Spooktacular' Stories."

Materials:

house pattern on colored construction paper
ghost pattern on white construction paper
scissors
glue
stapler

Directions to the student:

1. Choose a color and cut out a house pattern.
2. Cut out the ghost patterns.
3. Glue the ghosts to the house as shown.
4. Staple your story behind the house.

15

BOOK WEEK PUPPY

Feature some four-legged friends during National Children's Book Week in November. Share *How A Book Is Made* by Aliki for this occasion. Your students will be fascinated to learn about the process of printing a book.

Discuss favorite books students would like to share with classmates. Then create the reading pup project with the patterns on pages 18–19 to frame book reports. (Younger students can label the colored book cover with a favorite title and author.) Mount the finished projects on a bulletin board with the title "We're Barking About Good Books!"

We're Barking About Good Books!

Title: Alexander And The Wind-Up Mouse

Author: Leo Lionni

Main Character:
Alexander
Willy
the magic lizard

Setting:
This story takes place at Annie's house and in the garden.

My Favorite Part:
I liked the part where Willy gets changed into a real mouse!

Materials:

8½" x 11" rectangle of colored construction paper
book report form on white copy paper
dog patterns on white, brown, or black
    construction paper
scissors
glue
crayons

Directions to the student:

1. Write your book report on the form and cut it out.
2. Glue your report to the construction-paper rectangle and trim it to match the book shape.
3. Cut out the dog's head, paws, and tail, and glue to the book as shown.

Book Pattern

Title: _____

Author: _____

Main Characters: _____

Setting: _____

My Favorite Part: _____

THANKFUL TURKEY

Let students strut their stuff with this Thanksgiving display! Read *A Turkey For Thanksgiving* by Eve Bunting to your students. Mrs. Moose tells her husband she wishes she had a real turkey for Thanksgiving like everyone else. When Mr. Moose returns with Turkey, the guest is thankful that he is *at* the table and not *on* it!

After sharing the book, ask your students to make lists of things for which they are thankful. Then use the patterns on pages 21–22 to create the turkeys for a fine-feathered display titled "Grateful Gobblers."

As a variation on the directions below, have students write short paragraphs describing why they are grateful this Thanksgiving. Attach each student's paper beneath the turkey's wings.

Materials:

turkey patterns on colored construction paper
feather patterns on colored construction paper
scissors
glue
crayons

Directions to the student:

1. Cut out the turkey body, head, and feet, and glue them together as shown.
2. Cut out seven feathers.
3. Glue the feathers to the back of the turkey.
4. Write the words "Things I Am Thankful For" on the turkey body.
5. Label each feather with something for which you are thankful.

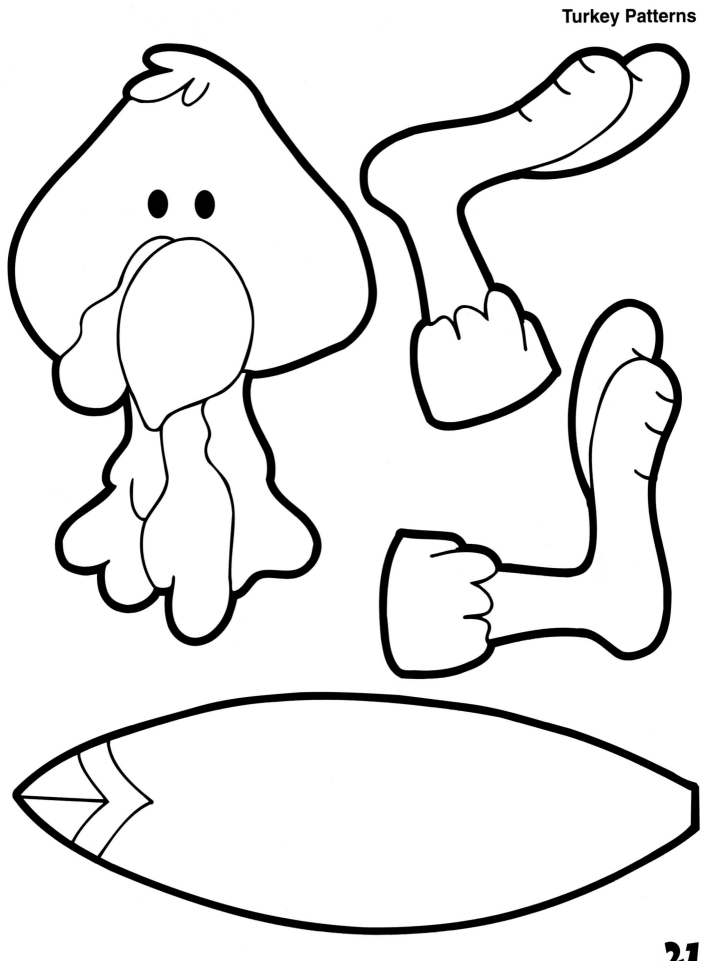

Turkey Patterns

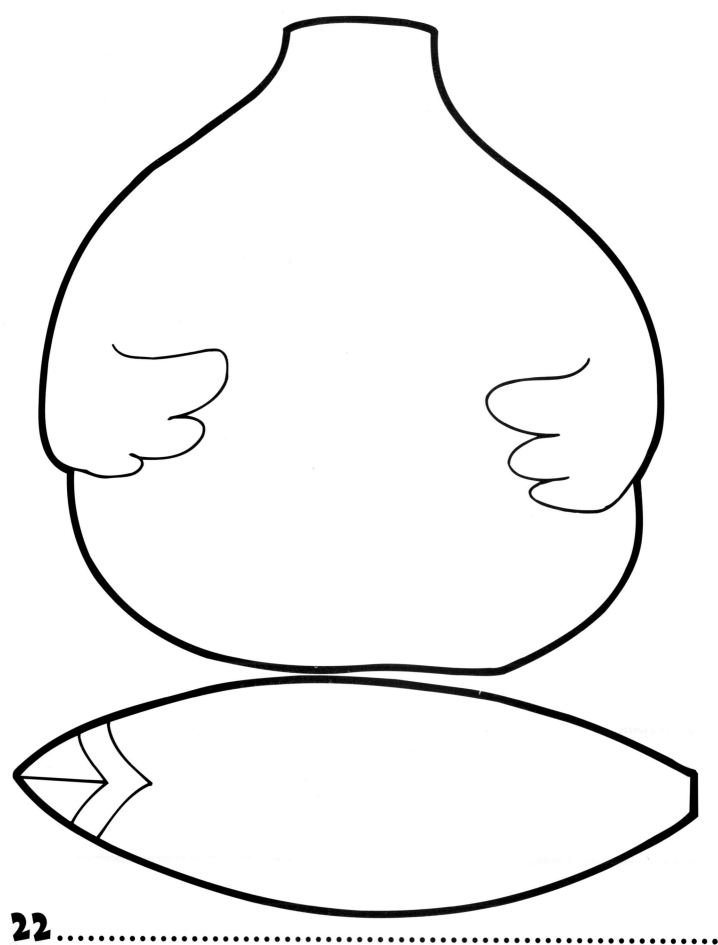

22

MERRY MOUSE

Celebrate the season with these merry mice! Share *The Song Of The Christmas Mouse* by Shirley R. Murphy. On Christmas morning, Rick and his cousin Hattie Lou share the excitement of seeing a little mouse on their Christmas tree.

Invite students to create these tree-trimming mice with holiday greetings or as accents for seasonal poetry. Use the patterns on pages 24–25.

Merry Christmas, Mom and Dad!

♥

I love you, Chris

Materials:

ornament pattern on colored construction paper
mouse patterns on white or gray construction paper
pink construction-paper scraps
12" x 18" sheet of red construction paper
6" circle of white copy paper
scissors
glue
crayons

Directions to the student:

1. Cut out the ornament pattern.
2. Cut out the mouse patterns and glue to the ornament as shown.
3. Add pink paper scraps to the mouse's ears.
4. Fold the red paper to make a card.
5. Glue the ornament and mouse to the front of the card.
6. Write a message or poem on a circle of white paper. Glue your writing to the ornament.

Ornament Pattern

24 . . . .

RUDOLPH'S WANT ADS

'Tis the season for reindeer and writing when your students create these adorable versions of Rudolph! Share the original version of the tale, *Rudolph The Red-Nosed Reindeer* by Robert L. May.

After sharing the story, discuss with students how Santa always needs extra help at Christmastime. Have each student write a want ad for a job to help Santa. Encourage students to think of humorous or unusual jobs rather than obvious ones. Then have them construct paper versions of Rudolph, using the patterns on page 27, to show off their advertisements. Place the completed projects on a bulletin board titled "Holiday Help Wanted."

HELP WANTED

Reindeer Groomer: Must like cold temperatures. Be tall enough to polish antlers. Benefits include frequent flyer miles, summers off, and milk and cookie breaks.

Holiday Help Wanted

Materials:

reindeer patterns on brown construction paper
white copy paper
shiny red wrapping paper
scissors
glue
markers

Directions to the student:

1. Write your ad on the white paper.
2. Cut out the reindeer patterns.
3. Glue the reindeer head and hooves to the copy paper as shown.
4. Glue on a circle of red wrapping paper for Rudolph's nose.

NEW YEAR CELEBRATION

It's the time of year for revelry and resolutions! Read *Un-Happy New Year, Emma!* by James Stevenson. Emma the witch resolves to be extra-nice to her friends, Dolores and Lavinia, in spite of the fact that they play mean tricks on her. When her witchy friends continue their pranks, Emma gets even with a plan of her own.

Help my Mom and Dad more.
Eric

Walk my dog, Rusty, every day.
Sarah

Read Our Resolutions

Be nice to my brother.
Wanda

After reading the story, discuss New Year's traditions with students. Ask them to think of some resolutions for things they would like to do for the year. Create the hat and balloon cutouts, using the patterns on pages 29–30. Display the written resolutions on a bulletin board with the title "Read Our Resolutions!"

Materials:

hat and balloon patterns on colored construction
  paper
scissors
markers
curling ribbon

Directions to the student:

1. Cut out a hat or balloon pattern.
2. Write one or more of your New Year's resolutions on it.
3. Add strips of curling ribbon to the top of your hat, or use the ribbon to create a string for your balloon.

29

Balloon Pattern

30 . . . .

SMILING SNOWMAN

Snowflake
Delicate, fragile
Swirls, dances, floats
Soft, peaceful, calm, cold
Snowstar

Have students welcome winter weather with seasonal cinquains and frosty friends. Read *Bob The Snowman* by Sylvia Loretan, the story of an adventurous snowman who decides to travel south on a train. Bob goes through some interesting changes before returning home to a whole family of snowpeople!

Ask students to think of other images of winter weather—snowmen, snowflakes, mittens, hot chocolate, etc. Then show them the pattern for writing a cinquain similar to the example:

Name of poem (one noun, or naming word)
How it looks (two adjectives, or describing words)
What it does (three verbs, or action words)
Your thoughts about it (four words)
Synonym for name (one noun)

Have each student compose a cinquain about a favorite winter image. Then create the snowmen to display their poetry. Use the patterns on pages 32–33. Duplicate the top hat pattern on tagboard and cut it out to provide a template for students to trace.

Materials:

snowman head pattern on white construction paper
circle pattern on dark blue construction paper
scarf pattern on colored construction paper
brown construction paper
black construction paper
scissors
white paper doily
glue
materials for facial features (scraps, popcorn, or markers)

Directions to the student:

1. Cut out the snowman head, circle, and scarf.
2. Glue the doily to the circle for the snowman's body.
3. Tear arms from brown construction paper.
4. Glue the pieces together as shown.
5. Add facial features.
6. Trace and cut out a top hat from black paper and glue in place.
7. Glue your winter cinquain to the snowman's body.

Snowman Head And Hat Patterns

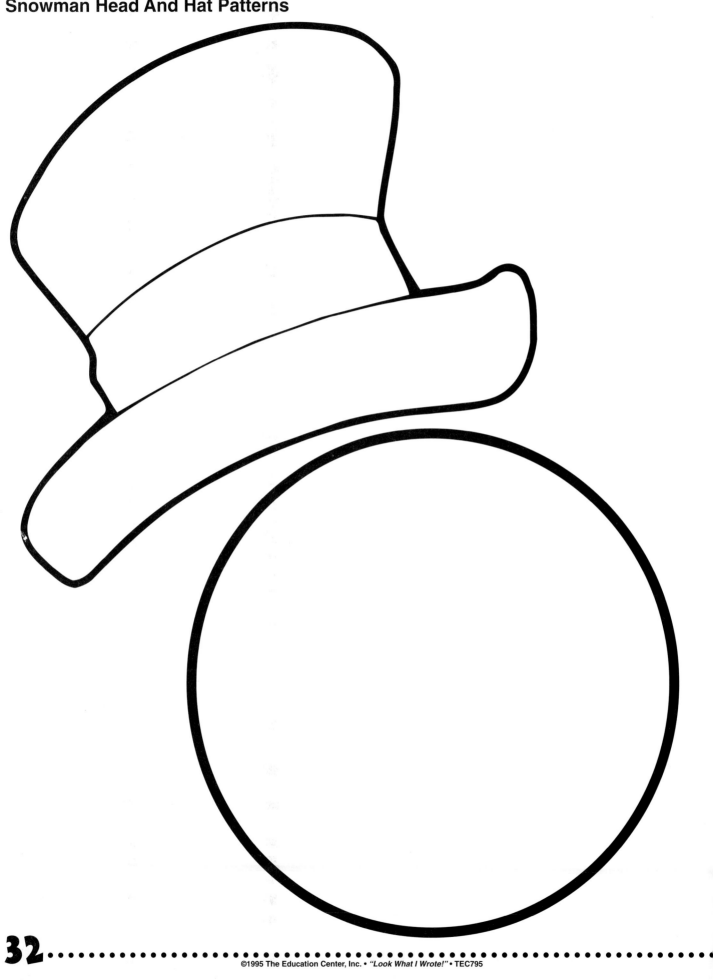

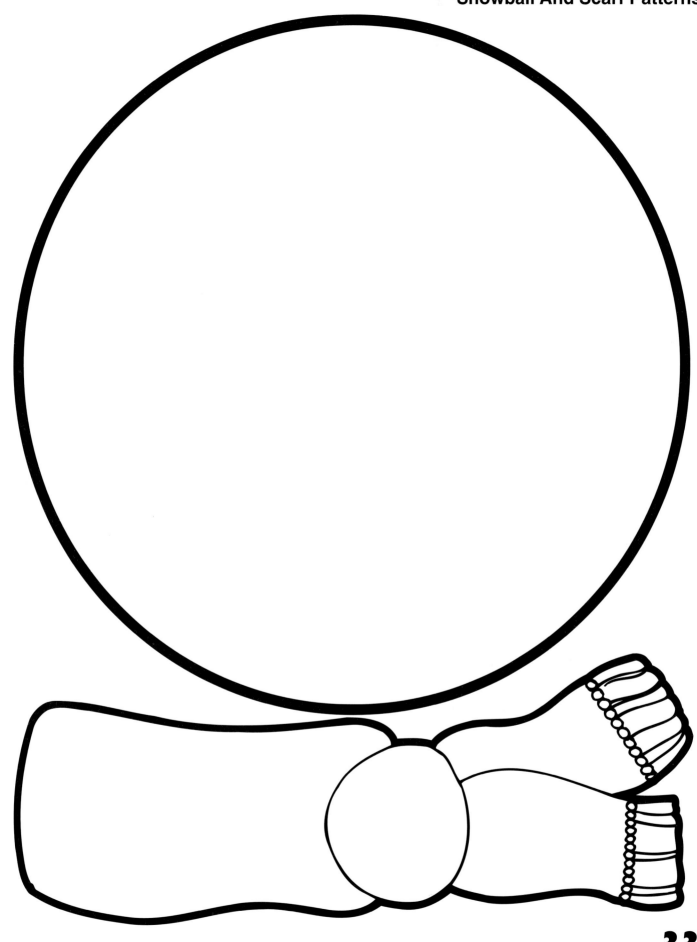

·········· TOOTH FAIRY FUN ··········

Keep track of lost teeth with a tooth fairy display. Read *The Tooth Witch* by Nurit Karlin, a book about the tooth witch who is tired of her job. The other witches call on a small witch to help her. After the tooth witch breaks her broom, the other witches send her on vacation. They send her helper to pick up a bag of teeth the tooth witch left on the moon. The small witch thinks that the teeth should be stars, so she places them in the sky. As she does so, she grows wings, her dress becomes white, and her broom turns into a wand. She becomes a fairy—the tooth fairy!

Josh Teal

I lost a tooth on...
Sept. 12   Jan. 3

After reading the story, have each child create a tooth cutout using the patterns on pages 35–36. Label the tooth with the student's name and note dates on which teeth are lost. Display them throughout the year with the title "Have You Lost A Tooth Today?" As a variation, have students write stories about what the tooth fairy does with the teeth she collects. Mount the stories on the tooth cutouts.

Materials:

tooth fairy pattern on colored construction paper
wand on yellow construction paper
tooth on white construction paper
scissors
glue
markers
stapler (optional)

Directions to the student:

1. Cut out the tooth fairy, wand, and tooth.
2. Glue the pieces together as shown.
3. Write your name on the tooth, or staple your story to the tooth.

34 ··························

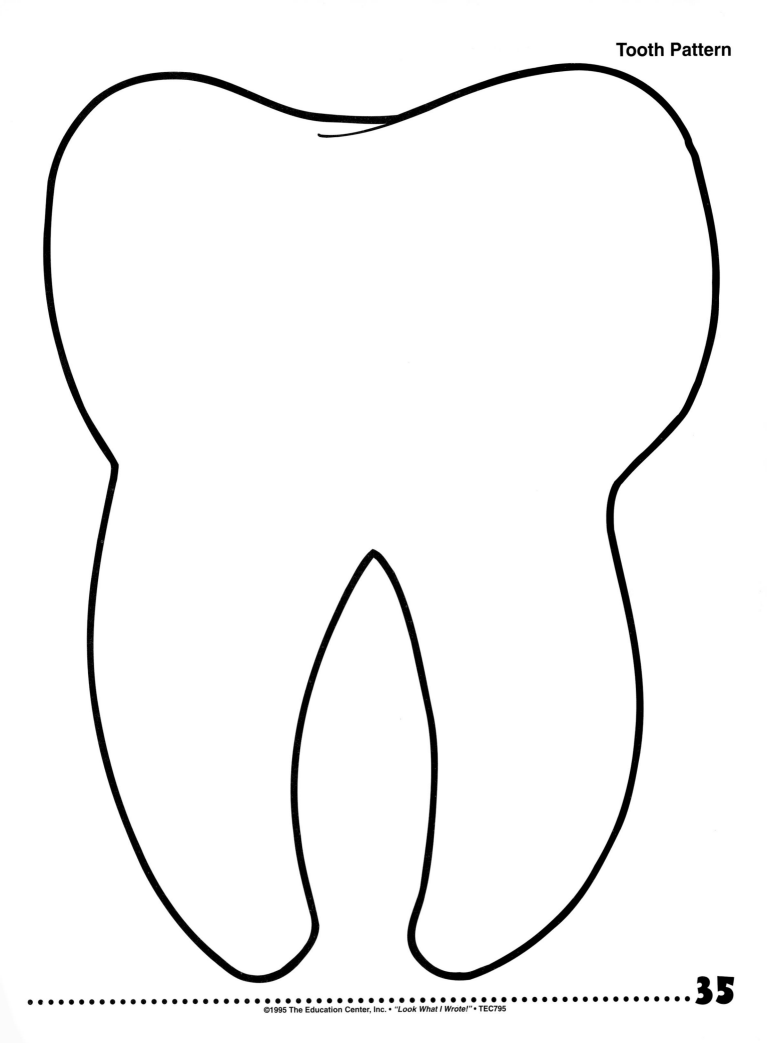

Tooth Fairy And Wand Patterns

36..

Take note of Groundhog Day on February 2 with stories displayed by this cute critter. Read *A Garden For A Groundhog* by Lorna Balian. The O'Learys plan a special garden for their groundhog in exchange for his prediction of the weather.

Mr. Groundhog lives in my neighbor's backyard. He has a wife named Greta and three children, Gloria, Greg, and Gil.

After sharing the book, have students create a shadow-seeking groundhog using the patterns on pages 38–39. Ask them to write stories about Mr. Groundhog, his family, and whether he sees his shadow. Mount the stories below the groundhog's shadow and add them to a display titled "Shadowy Stories."

Materials:

9" x 12" sheet of white construction paper
black construction paper
groundhog patterns on brown construction paper
sun pattern on yellow construction paper
white and beige construction-paper scraps
scissors
glue
stapler (optional)

Directions to the student:

1. Tear the edges of the white paper to resemble snow-covered ground.
2. Cut a black oval and glue it to the center of the white paper to represent the groundhog's hole.
3. Cut out the groundhog's face and paws; add scraps of white construction paper for teeth, and beige for muzzle and inner ears.
4. Glue the groundhog's head to the white paper so it looks as if he is peeking from the hole.
5. Tear a shadow from black paper and glue it on as shown.
6. Cut out the sun and glue it behind the white paper as shown.
7. Glue or staple your story below the shadow.

Groundhog Patterns

VALENTINE BEAR

Create a lovely display of students' work with these huggable bears! Read *The Valentine Bears* by Eve Bunting, a story of two bears who wake up from their hibernation to celebrate Valentine's Day. Mrs. Bear writes Mr. Bear two poems, so invite children to compose their own poems for someone special.

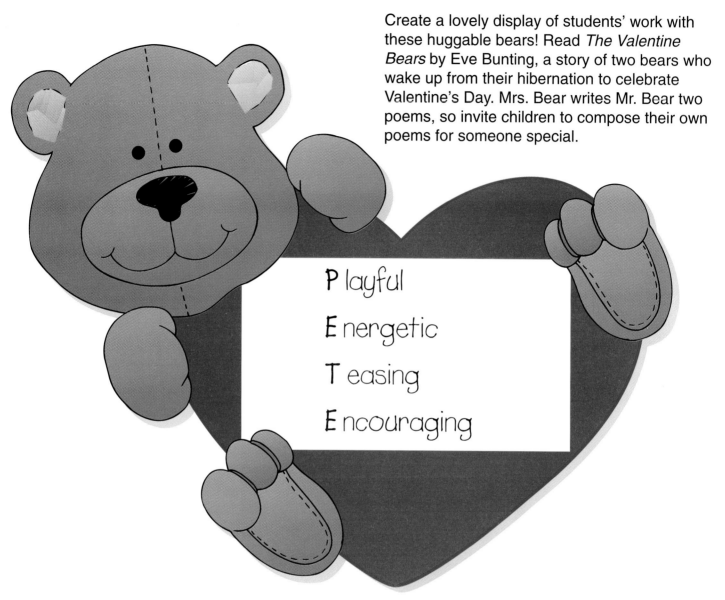

P layful
E nergetic
T easing
E ncouraging

Teach your students how to write an acrostic similar to the example, using a descriptive word beginning with each letter of a special person's name. Then have each child create a valentine bear using the patterns on pages 41–42. Mount the students' finished poems on the hearts and display the bears on a bulletin board with the title " 'Beary' Special People."

Materials:

heart pattern on red construction paper
bear patterns on brown construction paper
pink construction-paper scraps
scissors
glue

Directions to the student:

1. Cut out the heart pattern.
2. Glue your paper to the heart.
3. Cut out the bear head and paws, and glue them to the heart as shown.
4. Add pink paper scraps to the bear's inner ears.

Teddy Bear Patterns

42 •••

MEET MR. LINCOLN

Create a tip-top display for Presidents' Day! Read *President's Day* by Laura Alden. Carey and her class receive a visit from two men dressed as Abe Lincoln and George Washington. Discuss with the students what it might be like to meet Mr. Lincoln or any other president. Then have them write what they would say to Mr. Lincoln if he were alive today. Have each child create Abe Lincoln using the patterns on pages 44–45. Duplicate the beard pattern on tagboard and cut out for students to use as a template. Mount student papers on the top hats and display the finished projects on a bulletin board titled "Dear Mr. Lincoln."

Dear Mr. Lincoln,
Why do you wear a top hat? And why did you grow a beard? Does it itch?

Materials:

6" x 8" sheet of black construction paper
1" x 8" strip of black construction paper
face pattern on beige construction paper
black construction paper
scissors
glue
stapler (optional)

Directions to the student:

1. Glue the strip of black paper along one short side of the sheet of black paper to create a brim for Lincoln's top hat.
2. Cut out the face pattern. Trace the beard pattern on black construction paper and cut it out. Glue them together as shown.
3. Glue the face to the top hat as shown.
4. Staple or glue your paper to the top hat.

43

Mr. Lincoln Pattern

Glue beard here.

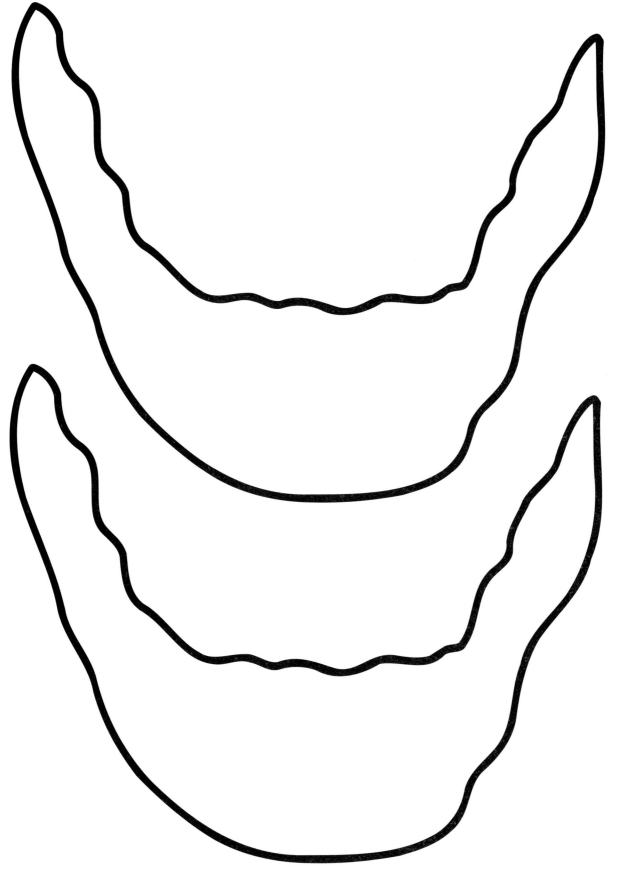

LEPRECHAUN'S POT OF GOLD

Celebrate St. Patrick's Day with these lucky leprechauns! Read *Leprechauns Never Lie* by Lorna Balian, the story of Ninny Nanny and Gram, who live together in an old thatched hut. The chores never get done until Ninny Nanny catches a leprechaun. Ninny Nanny does all the chores while the leprechaun tries to remember where he hid his gold. Finally she gives up on him and lets him go. When Ninny Nanny and Gram fall asleep, the leprechaun finds his gold and runs away.

I would hide my gold in the freezer. If a leprechaun tried to steal it, I'd freeze him in an ice cube!

Ask each child to think of where he could hide a pot of gold at his house. Have the students write stories describing their hiding places. Create leprechaun cutouts using the patterns on pages 47–48. Duplicate the pot pattern on tagboard and cut it out for students to use as a template. Then mount the students' writing on the pots of gold and display them with the title "Our Stories Are As Good As Gold."

Materials:

pot template
black construction paper
coin patterns on yellow construction paper
leprechaun on white construction paper
scissors
glue
white crayon
stapler (optional)

Directions to the student:

1. Trace and cut a pot shape from black construction paper.
2. Cut out the coins and glue them to the pot shape as shown.
3. Cut out the leprechaun and color him as desired.
4. Glue the leprechaun to the pot as shown.
5. Staple or glue your paper to the pot.

Pot Pattern

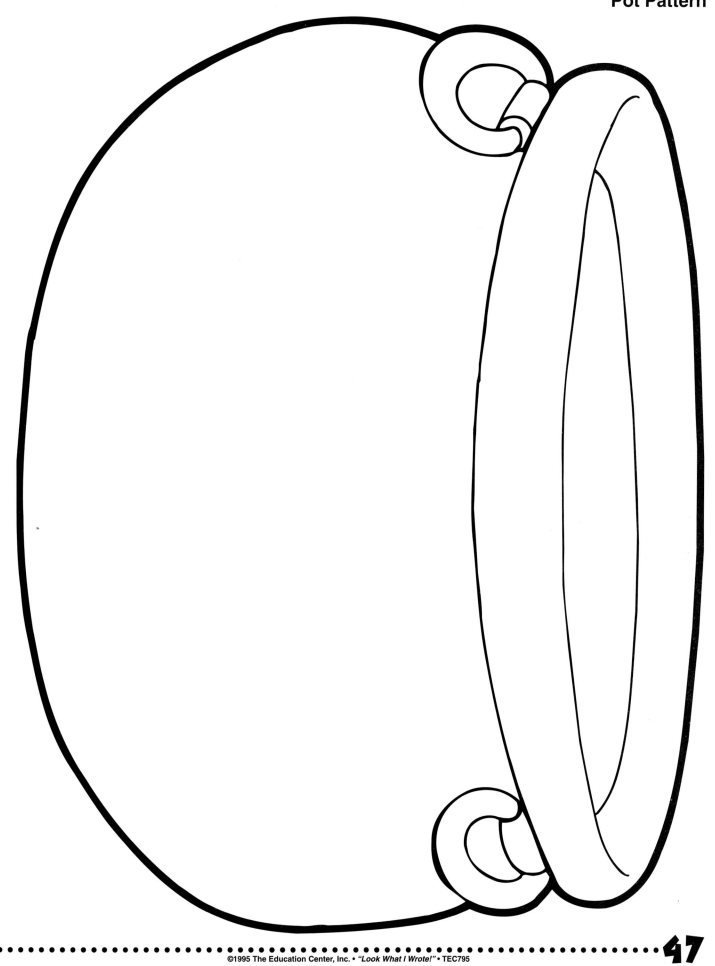

MY WONDERFUL WISHES...

I wish I could eat pizza every day.

I wish I had a new bike.

I wish I had a little sister.

I wish I could visit China.

I wish I could keep an alligator in my bathtub.

Myles

May All Your Wishes Come True!

This colorful display is what you've been wishing for! Read *Sylvester And The Magic Pebble* by William Steig, in which Sylvester finds a magic wishing pebble, but runs into some problems with his wishes. After reading the story, discuss some of your students' wonderful wishes. Have each child create a wishing rainbow using the patterns on pages 50–51. Each student should write one wish on each band of her rainbow. Display the rainbows on a bulletin board titled "May All Your Wishes Come True!"

Materials:

rainbow pattern on white construction paper
cloud pattern on white construction paper
bird pattern on blue construction paper
scissors
marker
crayons

Directions to the student:

1. Cut out the rainbow pattern.
2. Color the top band of the rainbow red.
3. Use a dark marker to write one wish on each remaining band of the rainbow.
4. Color the bands below the red band in the following order: yellow, orange, green, blue, and violet.
5. Cut out the cloud and bird patterns, and glue them to the rainbow as shown.
6. Write your name on the cloud.

Rainbow Pattern

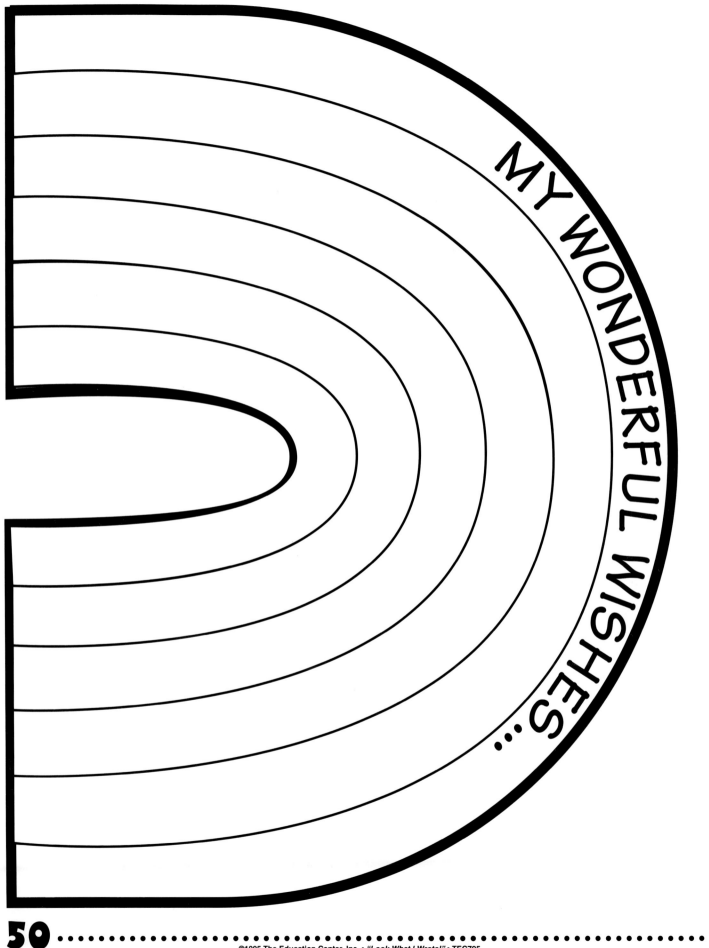

MY WONDERFUL WISHES...

Welcome spring with robins and wriggly worms! Read the book *Round Robin* by Jack Kent, the story of a robin who likes to eat so much he cannot fly south for the winter, so he hops instead. By the time he finds the other robins in the south, it is time to go north again.

Round Robin could have gone south on a bus.

After reading the story, brainstorm with students about various ways Round Robin could have traveled south besides flying or hopping. Give students some transportation examples to get them started; then provide them with 5" x 8" pieces of writing paper and let them write their own traveling adventures for Round Robin. Have students create the robin cutout using the patterns on pages 53–54. Then attach the students' stories to construction-paper "suitcases" and display them with the title "Welcome Back, Round Robin!"

Materials:

robin pattern on white construction paper
wing and handle pattern on white construciton paper
5¹/₂" x 8¹/₂" rectangle of colored construction paper
worm patterns on colored construction paper
white paper reinforcer
scissors
glue

Directions to the student:

1. Color and cut out the robin and wing patterns. Glue them together as shown.
2. Attach the paper reinforcer for the robin's eye.
3. Cut out a worm. Glue it to the robin's beak.
4. Attach your paper to the construction-paper rectangle and glue the "suitcase" to the handle as shown.
5. Glue a worm to the bottom of your paper.

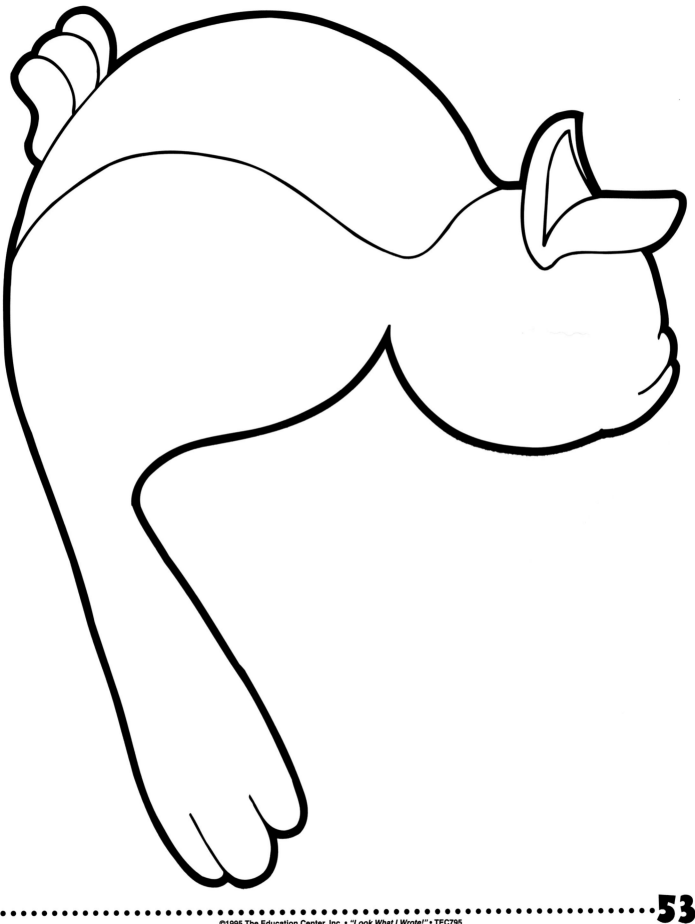

Wing And Worm Patterns

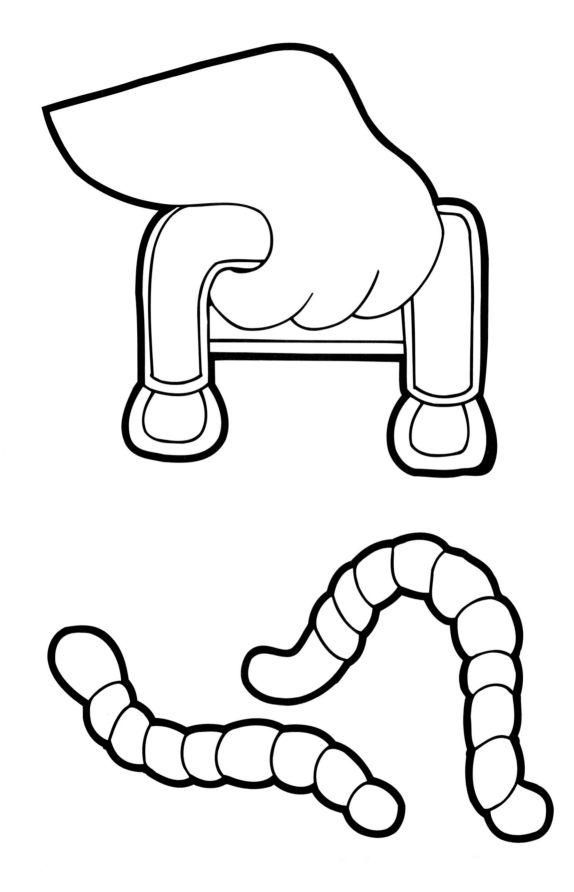

BUNNY'S BIG EGG

Usher in Easter with these enormous eggs! Read *The Easter Egg Artists* by Adrienne Adams. The Abbott rabbit family paints Easter eggs and many other things, too, in this delightful story. After reading the book, involve your students in writing their own haikus similar to the example. Tell students the "writing rules" for a haiku:

• a haiku always refers to nature
• a haiku is about a single topic
• a haiku never uses "I"
• a haiku does not rhyme
• a haiku follows a specific form:
  Line 1: five syllables
  Line 2: seven syllables
  Line 3: five syllables

Have students create the bunny using the patterns on pages 56–57. Mount each finished haiku on an Easter egg and display them with the title " 'Eggs-tra' Special Poetry."

A little rabbit
wiggles his tiny pink nose.
He smells the spring air.

Materials:

egg pattern on pastel construction paper
bunny head and body on white construction
  paper
pink construction-paper scraps
white cotton ball
scissors
glue
stapler (optional)

Directions to the student:

1. Choose a color of Easter egg and cut it out.
2. Cut out the bunny head and body, and glue them to the egg as shown.
3. Add pink paper scraps to the bunny's inner ears and nose.
4. Glue on a cotton-ball tail as shown.
5. Staple or glue your finished poem to the Easter egg.

Egg Pattern

56 •

THE "BERRY" BEST MOM

Take note of Mother's Day with this sweet idea! Read *The Mother's Day Mice* by Eve Bunting, the story of three mice who try to find the perfect gifts for Mother's Day. Biggest Mouse finds a dandelion fluff ball and Middle Mouse picks a juicy strawberry. Littlest Mouse is disappointed when he cannot get the gift he planned to give Mother. But he thinks of a gift that is even better!

You're the "Berry" Best Mom because you always let me help when you bake a cake!

Our Moms Are The Picks Of The Patch

Ask your students to think about why their moms are special to them. Have them create the strawberry cutout using the patterns on pages 59–60. Then have each student print an ending for the sentence on the berry. Display the finished cutouts in a "strawberry patch" complete with green tissue leaves. When the time is ripe, send them home for Mother's Day!

Materials:

strawberry pattern on red construction paper
strawberry top pattern on green construction
paper
scissors
glue
marker

Directions to the student:

1. Cut out the strawberry and top, and glue together as shown.
2. Use the marker to write the ending to the sentence.
3. Use black marker to add the strawberry seeds.

You're the "Berry"
Best Mom because

Strawberry Top Patterns

DAD'S DAY TEE

This project will fit dad to a "T"! Share *Happy Father's Day* by Steven Kroll, a story where everyone in the family has a special gift for dad. Then involve students in creating their own unique Father's Day presents.

Demonstrate for children how to create rebuses similar to the example. Then have them create T-shirts using the pattern on page 62. Have each child copy her rebus onto the shirt in pencil, then go over it with a marker or crayon. Display the finished shirts on a bulletin board titled "Tee Time For Dad" before sending them home for Father's Day.

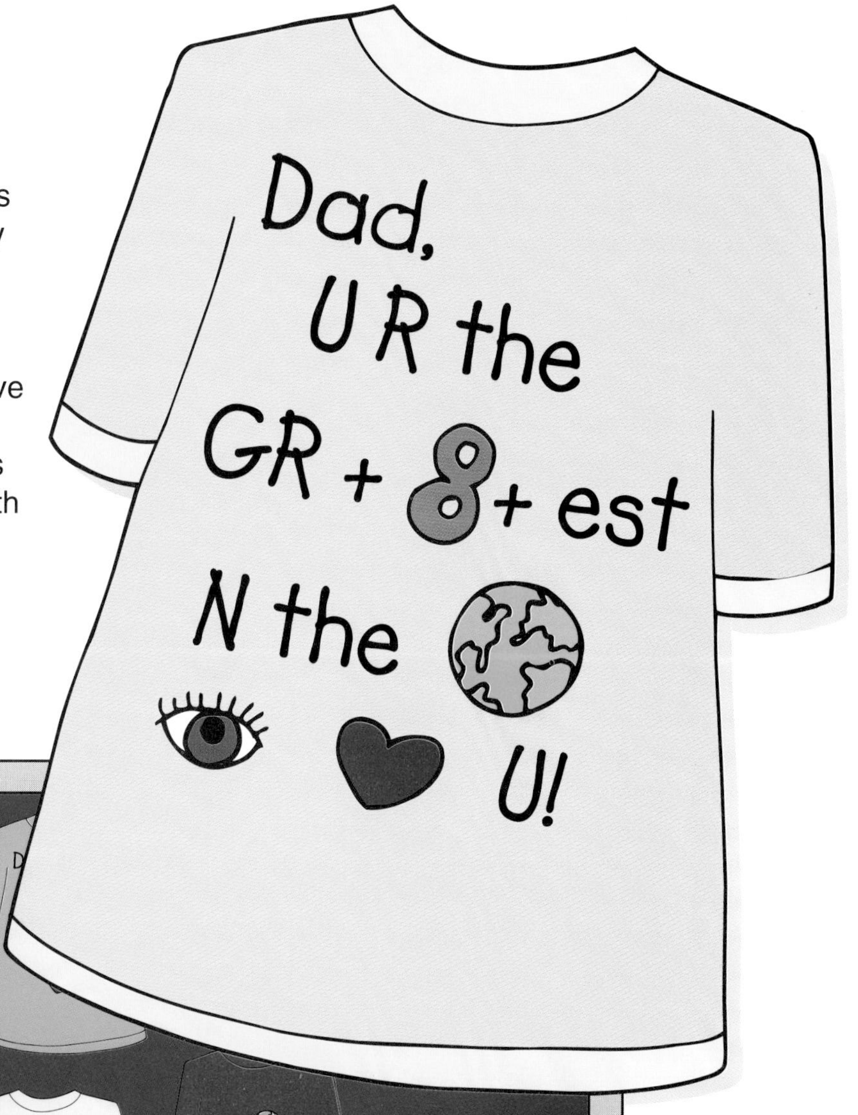

Dad,
U R the
GR + 8 + est
N the
U!

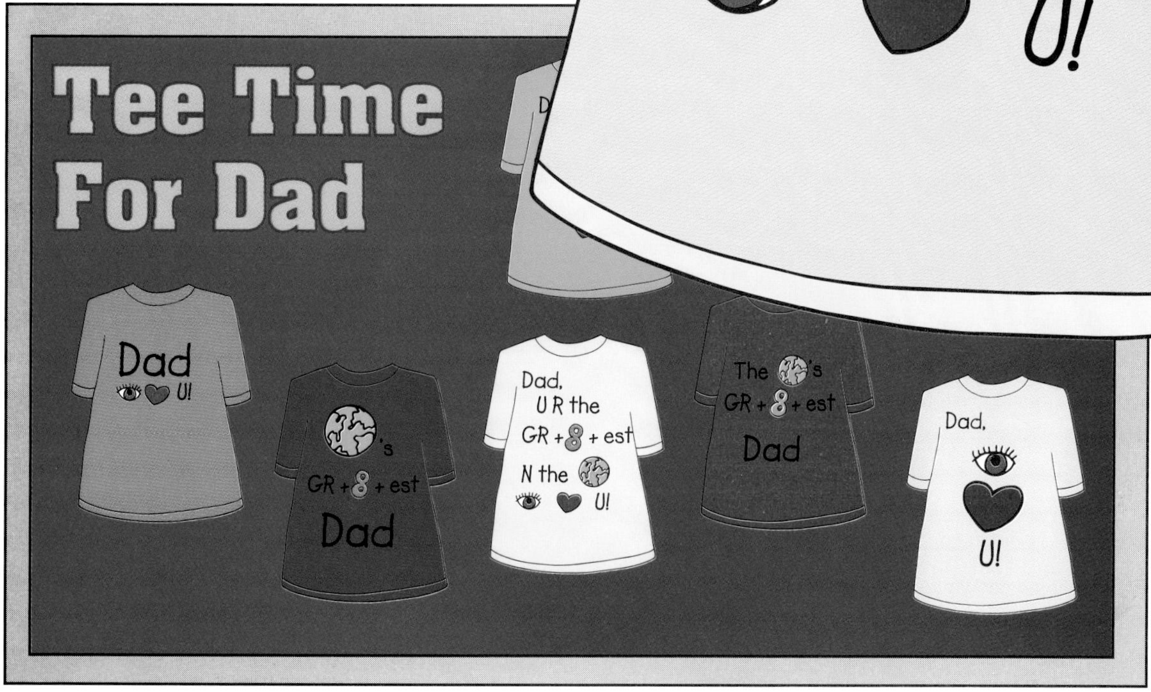

Tee Time
For Dad
Dad
U!
's
GR + 8 + est
Dad
Dad,
U R the
GR + 8 + est
N the
U!
The 's
GR + 8 + est
Dad
Dad,
U!

Materials:

T-shirt pattern on colored construction paper
scissors
pencil
marker or crayon

Directions to the student:

1. Choose a color and cut out the T-shirt pattern.
2. Copy your rebus onto the shirt in pencil.
3. Go over your writing with a marker or crayon.

T-shirt Pattern

62

······ FIRECRACKER FOR THE FOURTH ······

Put some bang into student writing with this firecracker display! Read *Henry's Fourth Of July* by Holly Keller. Henry, a rat, gets to stay up past his bedtime to watch fireworks for the first time in his life. After reading the story, discuss students' favorite activities for the Fourth of July. Then use the patterns on page 64 to create fantastic firecrackers! Demonstrate for students how to write an acrostic similar to the example, writing a descriptive word about the Fourth of July for each of the letters in the word *firecracker*. Display the completed firecrackers on a display titled "Firing Up For The Fourth!"

Fun
Independence
Revolution
Eating
Corn on the cob
Rides
Anthem
Cotton Candy
King George
Excitement
Red

Materials:

firecracker pattern on red construction paper
blast pattern on white construction paper
rat pattern on brown construction paper
short length of white pipe cleaner
red and blue glitter
scissors
glue
marker

Directions to the student:

1. Cut out the firecracker and blast patterns, and glue together as shown.
2. Glue the short length of pipe cleaner to the top of the firecracker as shown to represent the wick.
3. Cut out the rat pattern, and glue to the fire cracker.
4. Squeeze lines of glue over the blast pattern, and sprinkle on red and blue glitter.
5. Use the marker to write one word describing the Fourth of July for each letter in the word *firecracker*.

Firecracker Pattern